UNMUTED

RECLAIM YOUR VOICE

Book Cover: Muhammad Arslan

Formatted by: Samia Asif

Editor: Rachel McGee Beck, CoryShay Publishing

Dedication

To my WHY,
Dejah and Brielle.
Your unconditional love
helps me live fearlessly.
Mommy loves you!

TABLE OF CONTENTS

Introduction

For a long time, I didn't struggle to speak up—I struggled to see myself. I showed up, I worked hard and I poured into everyone around me. People saw something in me—potential, power, promise—but I couldn't always see it in myself. I questioned my worth, doubted my value, and assumed that pushing through was the same as being whole.

But surviving isn't the same as thriving; and being visible to others doesn't mean you feel seen by yourself.

Unmuted is the journey of closing that gap. This journal is my personal blueprint—the six steps I followed to shift from self-doubt to self-worth:

Self-Discovery

Self-Assurance

Self-Brand

Self-Development Plan

Self-Care

Self-Worth

These aren't just steps! They are the stages in my life that helped me unpack who I thought I had to be.

In order to step fully into the goddess I am becoming, I had to release the weight of people-pleasing and redefine my definition of success. Success that flows from my spirit...not society!

This six-step interactive journal will highlight the tools and roadmap I longed for when I was still searching for my own voice.

My hope is that by the time you finish this journal, you'll see yourself more clearly also...not as someone you've been told to be.

Instead you will see a more powerful, worthy, unmuted version of yourself and discover... that it's not just about finding your voice. No way! It's about finally unmuting the one you've always had!

So get your pen ready, because this powerful journal is filled with reflection and homework.

The Path to your Best Self

Have you ever heard how people have created the life of their dreams, because they started drinking the "kool-aid" of self-belief. They did things like create healthy habits, or read that life changing book. They decide to go to therapy, or they stop doing the things that held them back. I call this doing the work, and these people we see, know or have heard of, were able to believe just enough to transform their lives. Consider this your first step towards your dream life!

I will take you through my personal journey, one that took three years to get me to a place I call self-worth. My journey to self-worth rewards me the opportunity to live the life of my dreams. It resulted in me doubling my income, starting a consulting business, becoming a podcaster, leaving a toxic marriage, healing my inner child, traveling internationally and publishing my first book.

I am no stranger to helping. My core strengths are connecting and teaching. I am an award-winning IT professional with over fifteen years of experience, specializing in global strategic initiatives and technical program management. Besides my professional achievements, I've been awarded the opportunity to mentor junior and mid-career professionals, friends and family, resulting in promotions, new jobs and stronger leadership relationships. I am passionate about partnering with others to achieve their success, while empowering them in their career journey. May this journal inspire you to live the life of your dreams, because you are worthy!

SELF-DISCOVERY

After having my second daughter, I felt a heavy financial burden and a push to make more money. Filled with determination to figure it out, I responded to an email my vice president sent. I asked her if she was open to meet with me. My goal was to not only connect and expand my network, but to also seek advice. I was curious as to how women can be successful in their career, and also be a good wife and mother. Since I had never formally met with her before, I did not know if she was married or even had children. So actually, asking for advice, was a leap of faith. I shared in a rather candid conversation my conflict of focusing on my career and being a good wife and mother. I asked her, "why do I feel like I have to choose?" The answer she gave me changed my life. Her words were "you can have it all!"

Those words still echo in my ear. They were the words I never knew I needed to hear, yet were required to get me off my ass. "You can have it all." As I close my eyes, the words will forever have a crescendo effect on me. "You can have it all." The darkness that consumed my closed lids, allowed me to listen to the voice within. The words that were forgotten, that never quite made it to the forefront of my mind. Yet, after hearing those five words, I had hope! Hope lit a firestorm within me spiraling me on a journey searching for that voice. Hence, my journey began. I call this self-discovery.

So how do you know if you are ready for your self discovery?

Consider this: you want to live a fulfilled life, but have no idea what that looks like. You are seeking happiness, but what does happiness mean to you? You are desperate for more, but you're unaware of how to make it happen.

It's the desperation of becoming that pushes you into an alignment of discovery. The enlightenment is discovering that your personal belief system has to change, it's a paradigm shift. This shift pushes you out of your comfort zone and whispers, "enough, it has to change!" The biggest thing that catapulted me in my journey, was the honest realization that I never dreamed past my fears. I knew I wanted things to make me feel accomplished, but I never felt like I was worthy of them. I also felt like those things would come at a price. I could get one, but I would lose the other. For example, if I wanted to grow in my career, what would it cost me? Would it cost me the price of being a good wife and mother? These thoughts plagued me, so I kept them in the back of my mind. I was too afraid to assimilate those choices, until I was forced!

It was the start of the pandemic, March 2020 when the words "you can have it all" gave me the courage I needed. With this newfound courage I put one foot in front of the other and started my journey. I needed to figure out what my all was. It empowered me to bulldoze my way into a place where I felt worthy of going. I went to find my "why."

Writing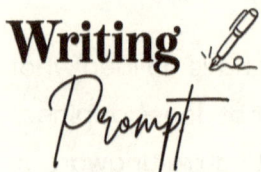
Prompt

Think back to a time when you felt a strong urge for change or growth in your life. What was the catalyst? Write about the moment that made you realize you needed to embark on a journey of self-discovery. If a moment hasn't happened for you yet, write down what you want to get out of this journal. What change(s) are you seeking for your life?

_____

_____

_____

_____

_____

_____

_____

_____

_____

_____

_____

_____

Writing
Prompt

What are you avoiding and how might they hold the key to your growth? What would your life look like if you fully embraced your authentic self?

Self- Reflection

Self-Reflection: Write down the first few words that come to mind, as you read the below questions. (In the below boxes)

What do I value most?
Am I living by these values?

When do I feel most
authentic and alive?

What fears are holding me
back from growth?

How do I define success
and happiness for myself?

Affirmations for Self-Discovery

Feel free to add any additional affirmations that come to mind.

Start each day by affirming your worth out loud. Stand in front of a mirror and speak these affirmations with confidence. Write them in your journal, post them around your mirror, home or workspace, or say/sing them in the car. Repeat them daily. This practice will ground you and guide you through your self-discovery journey.

- I am open to exploring every part of who I am.

- I embrace growth, even when it feels uncomfortable.

- My journey of self-discovery leads me to my most authentic self.

- I have the courage to question old beliefs and create new ones that serve me.

- I honor my past, while focusing on my present and future.

- Every step I take brings me closer to understanding my purpose.

- I am worthy of the time and effort it takes to know myself.

- I trust the process of uncovering my unique strengths and passions.

- I release self-doubt and welcome clarity into my life.

- The more I discover about myself, the more empowered I become.

You've Got Homework!

Continue to speak life into yourself throughout your self-discovery journey. If you need some direction on where to go next, here are some helpful resources.

Take an assessment to understand your unique strengths.

Go to *https://www.google.com* and take one of the following assessments:

- The Gift of Standout

- Gallup Strengthsfinders

This will help you see your unique strengths, and how they can support you in identifying your why.

For the reading enthusiast, tap into one of my early reads that gave me great perspective, insight and inspiration.

- "Find Your Why: A Practical Guide for Discovering Purpose for You and Your Team" by David Mead, Peter Docker, and Simon Sinek

- "The Memo" by Minda Hart

Writing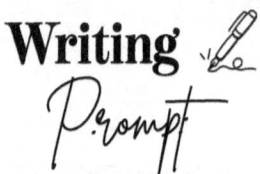
Prompt

What beliefs, habits or circumstances did you leave behind? What new perspectives or practices helped you shift your mindset? (Answer after completing the homework.)

SELF-ASSURANCE

The personal journey from self-discovery to self-assurance equated to five months for me. I was engulfed in reading two to three books a month and meeting with multiple mentors. I was able to listen, learn and identify ways to apply their teachings. I was all in!

It became clear, during this time that I deserved to make more money. The ability to make more income would put my family in a better financial position. Many may be shocked that it took me five months to believe I was deserving of making more money, but let me put it to you this way: I come from the narrative count your blessings. I was taught to be satisified with what you have, because you have what you need. If you asked for more, then some might say that you were unappreciative. I felt that I would be defying God by asking for more. I arrived at the understanding that I was promised an abundant life. I knew I was not going to prosper at my current income level. The discovery journey left me reading books and completing self-assessments that highlighted my personal and professional strengths, while calling out the areas I needed to work on. This realization gave me a boost! I was excited by my newly found confidence.

Self-discovery was filled with creating connections through coaching conversations with peers and leaders within the company

I work for. Many of those coaching conversations helped me to identify mentors, who not only shared their stories with me, but also gave me valuable insights. Some mentors later became sponsors.

Some of you may be new to the terms mentor, sponsor or coach so let me explain. Think of a coach as someone who has given you guidance over a particular situation. They may share best practices from experience and leave you with a lens of knowing how to handle a situation. The coaching sessions are not on-going, but imperative. In fact, coaching can help you to identify a good mentor. One way of knowing is how you feel after the conversation with your coach. Do you feel heard? Seen? Does their advice leave you at ease or make you tense? These are key signs to pay attention to. Lastly, have they extended an invitation to meet with you again?

Coaching can lead to mentoring, which can be a turning point when the teaching is applied.

With mentoring it is ongoing, you are sharing your wins, losses, areas of growth and actions. Your mentor is supporting and providing recommendations for your development. Hard conversations take place and realizations turn into successfully executed career plans.

When mentors see that your brand equates to success, and they have the ability to help, they become sponsors. Sponsors are people who advocate for you when you are not in the room. They can recommend you for a position or even hire you themselves.

In my case, that one conversation led to those five words "you can have it all!" They turned my VP from a coach into a mentor, and sponsor all within a few months. I took her and other mentors advice and applied it to all aspects of my life, personally and professionally.

My curiosity led me to insightful conversations. Those who shared their insights allowed me to understand that no two journeys look alike. One clear observation was how leaders stood out.

Most leaders had similar qualities: a high-level of self awareness and the ability to make clear decisions under pressure. They are also life-long learners, who enjoy shaping future leaders. I honed in on their positivity, read constantly and listened to uplifting music. This helped me to get clear on my brand, my elevator pitch and my why. I felt assured, self-assured!

I wanted to keep this confidence. My recipe for positivity became the thing I relied on, when things seemed chaotic. My affirmations became so ingrained that I began teaching my daughters their own affirmations.

I was driven to tackle anything that would help me to improve. I recall my assessments pointed out that I had a limited view point and challenged me to see things from a broader perspective. I quickly thought of how I could start incorporating this recommendation.

Feeling self assured, I was ready to step into a new path in my journey. It was time to start planning my next career move.

Writing
Prompt

Fill in the blank. This area should be a positive reflection of how you see yourself, while discovering self assurance. This is your time to talk to yourself to remind yourself that you are worthy of the life of your dreams.

I am most proud of:

_____

_____

_____

_____

_____

_____

_____

_____

_____

_____

_____

_____

_____

_____

My assessment results showed/taught me:

_____

_____

_____

_____

_____

_____

_____

_____

_____

_____

_____

_____

_____

_____

_____

_____

_____

_____

_____

_____

_____

_____

Writing
Prompt

How can I view current obstacles as opportunities for growth? What negative thoughts about myself can I reframe into empowering ones?

Self Discovery has shown me:

_____

_____

_____

_____

_____

_____

_____

_____

_____

_____

_____

_____

_____

Affirmations for Self-Assurance

Begin each day speaking these affirmations. Stand in front of the mirror, write them down, place them around your work station, say or sing them when you are in the car, this will help you during your self-assurance journey. Feel free to add any additional affirmations that come to mind. Intertwine these self-assurance affirmations with your self-discovery affirmations.

- I trust in my abilities and my unique path.

- I am enough, just as I am.

- Challenges help me grow stronger and more confident.

- I am proud of how far I've come and excited for what's ahead.

- I release the need for external validation; my worth comes from within.

- I have everything I need to be successful.

- I am resilient, capable and worthy of success.

- My confidence grows with every action I take toward my goals.

- I honor my progress, even when it feels small.

- I choose to speak kindly to myself and celebrate my wins.

Reading: Self-Help Tip

SUGGESTED READINGS

"The Alchemist" By Paulo Coelho

"You Are A Badass" By Jen Sincero

Self Reflection Tips

- Build a professional network.

- Cultivate meaningful connections.

- Attend networking events.

- Join professional organizations.

- Engage in conversations, share knowledge.

- Seek advice from experienced professionals.

SELF- BRAND

What do you want to achieve? What are your dreams? Getting clear on your brand is going to help in answering these questions. After I completed the work in self-assurance, I had arrived at a place where I had to be clear on my why. I recall a transformative conversation I had with one of my mentors, when she asked "so, what's your next role?" I had no idea what role I wanted next, I just knew I desired more income. She asked, "what do you want to do? Better yet, what don't you want to do?" I laugh thinking about this now, because I knew I could make a list of what I did not want, so I compiled a list of don'ts. It led me to write a list of what I enjoyed doing in my career. The more I explored what I enjoyed, the clearer it became that my next role had to be more than just a title! I felt as though I was shopping for key ingredients that would lead to the perfect meal or in my case, the perfect role. Those key ingredients were made up of my strengths, passions and goals. My brand was a bag of awesome, unique qualities.

Now that I was clear on what my brand was, I pondered how I would articulate it. Since I had amazing mentors, I asked one of them for advice. I needed help deciphering how I should talk to my leader about a promotion. He suggested putting together a slide, so that I could visually present my current job family and description. I had to compare my current role to the role that was next level up.

The idea was to present the slide, emphasizing how I was already performing at the higher level, worthy of a promotion.

During a one-in-one meeting, I told my leader I felt ready for a promotion. He asked for me to schedule a separate meeting, to talk about it. As I mentally prepared, I not only took my mentor's advice to create a slide, I kicked it up a notch by creating seven additional slides. However, the last slide was not about my current role or job family.

Nope, it was a snapshot of me showcasing the things I love and my key attributes. It read: Strategic Initiatives; Program Management; Process Engineering and Operations. It was a sneak peek into the real me. It was completely different from the current role I had. The meeting felt more like a declaration conversation. One that I ensured would engage my audience of one. I curated a story of my why. I found a creative way to articulate my brand and to top it off, I had my leader's full support.

Here's how I built it:

Remember that homework I had you do? Now that you've unwrapped the insights from your assessments and unmuted your self-confidence, it's time to blend those newfound strengths into the essence of your identity. This is a key moment where you gather all the valuable information you've discovered about yourself and incorporate it into a refreshed resume with a captivating biography. This is your brand!

What's Next…

Consultant

Program Management

Process Improvement

Business Operations

Strategic Initiatives

Writing
Prompt

To know your brand, you have to know you. Think of it like painting a vibrant picture of your authentic self—one that not only highlights your skills and achievements, but also connects with the very core of who you are. So, let's turn those discoveries into a narrative that truly speaks volumes about your unique professional journey. Who are you?

_____

_____

_____

_____

_____

_____

_____

_____

_____

_____

_____

_____

_____

_____

Writing
Prompt

Is the way you see yourself an accurate reflection of how others perceive you, or are there hidden layers that only you understand? In what ways do you shape—or hide—your true self to influence how others see you? If you could control their perception entirely, what would you want them to see, and why?

Writing
Prompt

Reflect on who you are—your values, passions, and what makes you unique—while considering how you want others to perceive your brand. Then, craft a prompt (place this in an AI tool like ChatGPT or Copilot). Include key details about your personality and desired tone, such as: "Create a brand statement for me that is [fun/professional/creative], reflecting my personality as someone who is [adjectives]. Make it engaging and unique!" Once you receive a response, refine the wording to ensure it feels authentic and aligns with your personal or professional brand. Write it below:

_____

_____

_____

_____

_____

_____

_____

_____

_____

_____

_____

STEP | 4

SELF-DEVELOPMENT PLAN

Now is the time to go to work. Fair warning in order to get to self-worth and have the life of your dreams, you need to plan it. I do also believe in the law of attraction. You can attract it also, but in this case, we are going to plan for success.

In the ever evolving journey of my career, I found a compass in goal-setting. It wasn't just about envisioning the next step, it was about planning it. I was able to complete a development plan, which clearly outlined my strengths, or areas to strenghten. My goals, objectives and actions were to help me fill the gaps identified.

I created an action plan to address those areas to be strengthened and gave myself a timeline to do it. Either it being to develop my business acumen, lead an initiative, or complete courses for a certification. I held myself accountable to complete my goals by an assigned due date I gave myself. I also started sharing my plan with my leader, as I journeyed to figure out how to get to this new role.

Filled with determination, I found out I was accepted into a career development program. This program was internally ran by the company I work for. It was a culmination of professionals teaching you how to develop business acumen, how to have career conversations with your leader, and finding your why. Funny, these are the same things I had discovered while I was walking into my journey. However, this took it up a few levels and I learned much more than I ever imagined.

One of the events of the program awarded us the opportunity to get career advice via Zoom, from an executive leader. The roundtable introductions were held in November 2020. I was the only one prepared with a self-development plan. I walked them through some of the work I was doing and where I saw myself going in three to five years. My goal was to be transparent with the executive, so he could share steps on navigating to my next role. Little did I know, just how valuable that conversation would be, because it bought change to my career for the better.

My creative endeavor to create a slideshow would serve as the blueprint for my next role. About a month after that conversation, I got a chat notification from a coworker, whose name I recognized from the development program. In fact, it was the same coworker who sat in that Zoom meeting with the executive. He told me that he thought I would be a good fit for a role in his organization and wanted to know if I would speak to his director about it. This was not an interview; it was a pre-interview, which is even better—a preview of the real thing. This would be a complete advantage if everything went well.

Through the synergy of all the work I had done from self-discovery to self-development planning, I had manifested my next opportunity. I not only secured the position, but gained a title that echoed the essence of my slide show. It's proof that with a clear vision, a touch of creativity, you can truly manifest your dreams. I landed a role as a Global Strategic Initiative Program Manager. My role was to support the process improvement in the Portfolio Management

Operations organization. I mean I had these words on my slide and you mean to tell me there was a role out there that checked every box. Everyday I'm still amazed by the turn of events.

Writing *Prompt*

Imagine your ideal life five years from now—where are you, what are you doing, and how do you feel? Now, what's the very first step you can take today to bring that vision closer to reality?

_____

_____

_____

_____

_____

_____

_____

_____

_____

_____

_____

_____

_____

_____

_____

_____

_____

_____

Writing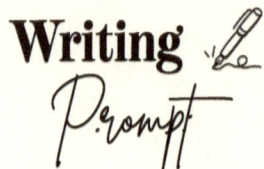
Prompt

What does success truly look like for you, beyond money and titles?

_____

_____

_____

_____

_____

_____

_____

_____

_____

_____

_____

_____

_____

_____

_____

_____

_____

_____

_____

Career Development Plan

Career Goals | List goals below that will lead to your dream position.

0-12 Months:

1-2 Years :

3-5 Years:

Growth Prospective | List the areas/skills needing developing?

Stand Out Qualities | List the areas/skills you excel in

Goal Gaps| Write down each area you listed in growth prespective (above)

Experience| Describe how this gap impacts your goal.

-
-
-

Action Plan

List the action(s) you will take to develop/fill the Gap	Objective/Related Gap	Due
Action 1:		
Action 2:		
Action 3:		

Career Development Plan

Career Goals | List goals below that will lead to your dream position.

0-12 Months:

1-2 Years :

3-5 Years:

Growth Prospective | List the areas/skills needing developing?

Stand Out Qualities | List the areas/skills you excel in

Goal Gaps| Write down each area you listed in growth prespective (above)

Experience| Describe how this gap impacts your goal.

- _____   _____
- _____   _____
- _____   _____

Action Plan

List the action(s) you will take to develop/fill the Gap	Objective/Related Gap	Due
Action 1:		
Action 2:		
Action 3:		

Career Development Plan

Career Goals | List goals below that will lead to your dream position.

0-12 Months:

1-2 Years :

3-5 Years:

Growth Prospective | List the areas/skills needing developing?

Stand Out Qualities | List the areas/skills you excel in

Goal Gaps| Write down each area you listed in growth prespective (above)

Experience| Describe how this gap impacts your goal.

-
-
-

Action Plan

List the action(s) you will take to develop/fill the Gap	Objective/Related Gap	Due
Action 1:		
Action 2:		
Action 3:		

Career Development Plan

Career Goals | List goals below that will lead to your dream position.

0-12 Months:

1-2 Years :

3-5 Years:

Growth Prospective | List the areas/skills needing developing?

Stand Out Qualities | List the areas/skills you excel in

Goal Gaps| Write down each area you listed in growth prespective (above)

Experience| Describe how this gap impacts your goal.

- _____ _____
- _____ _____
- _____ _____

Action Plan

List the action(s) you will take to develop/fill the Gap	Objective/Related Gap	Due
Action 1:		
Action 2:		
Action 3:		

5

Self-Care

The career development program played an instrumental role. It was the bridge to realizing my goal to contribute more money to the household. It was a year past that conversation that challenged me to go find my why. I came to the realization, I was worthy of having it all.

In my new role and environment, it was important to ensure that my inner-self found balance and that I heard my own voice and showed up authentically. I was rewarded a year of coaching, through the career development program, due to my significant role in the final team project.

The coaching program was through a company called Better Up. This part of my journey focused on evolving outside of the professional space. Yes, this was where we get to the root of me. The root of why my brand was so focused on solving complex problems, how I showed up as the mom, wife and friend. This part of the journey, scratched the surface of personal reflection in ways I never imagined. It all started with a question and an intense curiosity.

During my time on Better Up, I was introduced to a personal wellness coach, October 2021. Her goal was to ensure I practiced work-life balance. She provided clarity on how if not practiced, it could wreak havoc in my career. During one of our conversations, she asked me a profound question that resulted in another journey. "What do you do for self-care?" Self care, I thought. I responded "Self-care, what is that?" I had never heard of such a thing. I was focused on being a mother, wife and excelling in my career. Finding the time to pour into myself, outside of work, felt impossible. Unsure of where to start, my coach recommended I begin with painting, and to do it with my daughters. It was a great idea, that I quickly implemented.

It turned into a norm, paint night would be Fridays, which spilled over into color therapy and became a way for my mind to rest and be still. I found myself coloring before bed, it was my quiet time to connect with my inner thoughts. My daughters also wanted their own coloring books and color pencil sets. What started as a before bed routine, resulted in me coloring every chance I got. I eventually was able to have my time outside the house. Thursday evenings became my kid free evenings. My best friend and I enrolled into a Xtreme step class. These instances were some of my early moments of feeling free. I remembered what it felt like to experience new things and be open to change. This evolution of self care became something I wanted to experience more frequently, so I did self-care challenges.

Embracing self-care sharpened my awareness, allowing me to navigate my thoughts with greater clarity. This newfound clarity propelled me to take charge!

I crafted and executed a strategic plan to address work challenges. This was a move that marked a turning point in my professional trajectory. This success not only contributed significantly to boosting and refining my professional brand, but also positioned me as the optimal candidate for more advanced opportunities.

However, on the flip side my awareness became so clear that I realized that the space that surrounded me personally, was toxic. Yes, this is the part where I realized I was living in a marriage that was unreflective of what I was worthy of.

I recall a conversation with God in the summer of 2022, I said "I'm giving him thirty days, God show me that this is the marriage for me." I quickly heard a voice reply, "sixty days." Taken aback by the instinct of the number, I nodded in agreement. I started to observe how my husband acted, and the things he said. I thought about what I felt I deserved. I may write a book on the revelations during my nine-year marriage, and what it taught me about myself.

One thing is for sure, the self-care portion of this journey, forced me to look in the mirror and be honest with myself. Was I going to stay in a space I was not happy? Was I ready to make a change that would allow me to fully step into caring for myself? Did I even know how?

Self-care is about honoring your needs, setting boundaries, and creating a life that aligns with your well-being. Sometimes, caring for yourself can unmute areas of your life that no longer serve you. As I continued to execute my self-care plans, the more I realized I was in an area that no longer served me.

I was fully aware that my marriage did not support my mental well-being. It was also imperative that I set an example to my daughters, how a woman should be treated. It would take me another year before I had the courage to leave.

Writing
Prompt

Self-care as a concept:

When you hear the words "self-care," what thoughts or images come to mind?

How did your upbringing or past experiences shape how you viewed self-care?

_____

_____

_____

_____

_____

_____

_____

_____

_____

_____

_____

_____

_____

_____

_____

_____

_____

Writing ✒
Prompt:

What does self-care currently look like in your life?

How do you feel before and after you engage in self-care activities?

_____

_____

_____

_____

_____

_____

_____

_____

_____

_____

_____

_____

_____

_____

_____

_____

_____

_____

Writing
Prompt:

Reflect on a time when self-care led you to question a relationship, commitment, or belief you once had. What did you realize about yourself in that moment? Were there signs you had ignored before?

_____

_____

_____

_____

_____

_____

_____

_____

_____

_____

_____

_____

_____

_____

_____

_____

_____

_____

Self-Care Planner

DATE: _____ MONTH: _____ YEAR: _____

THINGS THAT MADE ME HAPPY TODAY

- _____
- _____
- _____

SELF-CARE ACTIVITIES

- _____
- _____
- _____
- _____

WATER INTAKE

TODAY'S MOOD

DAILY NUTRITION

Breakfast

Lunch

Dinner

Snacks

HABITS TO START

- _____
- _____
- _____
- _____
- _____
- _____

HABITS TO STOP

- _____
- _____
- _____
- _____
- _____
- _____

Self-Care Planner

DATE: _____   MONTH: _____   YEAR: _____

THINGS THAT MADE ME HAPPY TODAY

- _____
- _____
- _____

SELF-CARE ACTIVITIES

- _____
- _____
- _____
- _____

WATER INTAKE

TODAY'S MOOD

DAILY NUTRITION

Breakfast	
Lunch	
Dinner	
Snacks	

HABITS TO START

- _____
- _____
- _____
- _____
- _____
- _____

HABITS TO STOP

- _____
- _____
- _____
- _____
- _____
- _____

Self-Care Checklist

 *Self-care isn't an act but
a loving commitment to yourself.*

How did you cherish yourself this week? Did you:

☐ Take a long bath	☐ Engage in a hobby
☐ Read for pleasure	☐ Listen to your favorite music
☐ Go for a long walk	☐ Spend time with a loved one
☐ Practice mindful meditation	☐ Watch a light-hearted movie
☐ Journal your thoughts	☐ Pamper yourself
☐ Try gentle yoga	☐ Take a short nap
☐ Cook a nourishing meal	☐ Go for a swim
☐ Visit a museum or gallery	☐ Practice gratitude
☐ Gardening	☐ Attend a workshop or class
☐ Paint or draw	☐ Explore a new place

Self-Worth

I'll never forget Tuesday, June 20th 2023. That morning I woke up with so much clarity. I dreamt the night before and three images were revealed to me. The first image was an empty indoor swimming pool. The walls were a light tint of yellow and I recall seeing a tall, white lifeguard chair near the 6 ft sign.

The second image was in black and white. There was a grey concrete path in front of me. There were tall, black trees that created an arch. Darkness surrounded me, yet a glowing light appeared through the branches. There was a full moon illuminating the darkness.

The third image was a tall grey file cabinet. This image was in full motion. A drawer would open and inside was a box wrapped in string. After that, the drawer would close. Another drawer would open repeatedly and the same box followed.

I remember waking up after seeing these images and I knew. I could hear my inner voice say "abundance, not sacrifice." I could hear something saying "happiness, not hurt." Something in me woke up with enough strength to utter the words, " I want a divorce!"

I filed for divorce that Friday and also scheduled my first therapy appointment. Walking away from my marriage, was the moment that I stepped into self-worth.

Originally, I wanted to end this book right here. I've graduated to a place of self-worth, a space I want everyone to discover. It gives the feeling 'cheers, you have arrived!' When I sit in my backyard, I can hear my neighbor's fountain. The fountain brings a calmness over me and I have an "ah-huh" moment. I'm learning that self-worth isn't a destination, it's a journey! A journey I will spend my life continuously redefining and rediscovering, even though it's two years later.

Leaving my marriage taught me many lessons. The biggest one was: no more conforming to societal thoughts on how to live. No more people-pleasing! No more fighting for acceptance! No more fearing rejection! No more holding back! No more what- ifs! Most importantly, learning to live an authentic life on my own terms. After years of feeling like everything came at the expense of my own peace, I was finally the main character. I felt free! Little did I know my real journey of self -worth was just beginning.

At my first therapy appointment, I was asked how I felt. I told my therapist... I was fine, just fine! She looked at me puzzled and even though the appointment was virtual, I could feel her bewilderment through the screen. I wondered if I had said something wrong. It was during that appointment that I was diagnosed with High Generalized Anxiety Disorder.

I was emotionally disconnected with me. Honestly, I was scared to feel or have negative feelings. Could hurt lead to depression? Could anger cause me to make bad choices? I was too afraid to find out, but my therapist challenged me to tap into my feelings. I learned through cognitive behavioral therapy how to process my feelings. I journaled everything.

I found myself emerged in big emotions. When I was sad, crying or mad I worked out in the gym. When I was happy, I showed it by dancing.

Journaling became the place where I processed my feelings. The words I wrote honored my feelings and slowly helped me to find my voice. Social media turned into a place to reflect my happiness and highlight my freedom.

Social media became my video diary. Stepping into self-worth was electrifying! I wanted to shout it to the world. But the same freedom that set me free also tested me, leaving me exposed and trembling when I shared my most vulnerable video for all to see. I was preparing for divorce court the next day. Now with the ability to connect with my feelings, I was scared.

Since social media had become my outlet for expression, I shared my raw emotions. I needed to process the feelings I had out loud. I also felt like I owed it to the people who were cheering me on in the background. So I turned on my camera, hit record and uploaded me crying and explaining how I scared I was.

I felt a fire in my belly. A fire that my VP had ignited when she said "I could have it all." I knew that by sharing my experiences, both good and bad, other people would be helped. My experience would encourage and uplift so many. This was my purpose. I realized that my story is not for me, it's to be shared!

It wasn't long before text, phone calls, emails and DMs started to pour in. My community heard my cry and they responded. I heard so many amazing stories that week. Yes, I said that week! It took that long to respond to phone calls, text or direct messages. I never felt so loved or judged all at the same time.

With all of these complex emotions, I decided to become a content creator. As a content creator I would continue to share my story, connect, build bridges, change lives, support, love, be an ear and hold space for the spaceless.

You've arrived, you deserve so much more. My journey has evolved into a profound source of self-worth revealing eye-opening truths and inspiring transformative changes. In the professional sphere, I actively sought and obtained a new role. It was a testament to the respect and influence my brand commands.

Simultaneously, I find myself frequently invited to contribute to initiatives that resonate with my identity. This enables me to authentically express myself in my professional endeavors.

Integral to this journey is the passion infused into my work, it is a fulfilling reflection of my core being, that creates a continuous cycle of clarity. As I pause to reflect, the most powerful shift I made was creating my own belief system. Through meditation, prayer, therapy, life coaches, chakra cleansing, energy healing, and charging my crystals beneath the full moon, I became unmuted—cutting cords, releasing old ties, and stepping into profound peace. This peace has made the transformation real. One that continues to unfold and shape the more unmuted versions of who I am becoming. I am grateful I started my journey of being curious and believing I am worthy enough, to have it all.

Tips for Strengthening your Self-Worth

1. Practice Self-Compassion:
   a. Be kind to yourself, especially in moments of failure or difficulty.
   b. Treat yourself with the same kindness and understanding that you would offer to a friend.

2. Develop Positive Affirmations:
   a. Identify and challenge negative self-talk.
   b. Create positive affirmations to reinforce a healthy self-image.

3. Learn and Grow:
   a. Embrace a mindset of continuous learning and personal development.
   b. Focus on acquiring new skills and knowledge.
   c. Contributing to the well-being of others can foster a sense of purpose and accomplishment.

4. Take Care of Your Physical Health:
   a. Exercise regularly to boost mood and energy levels.
   b. Prioritize adequate sleep and maintain a balanced diet.

5. Mindfulness and Meditation:
   a. Practice mindfulness to stay present and reduce stress.
   b. Engage in meditation to foster self-awareness and inner peace.

6. Volunteer or Help Others:
   a. Contributing to the well-being of others can foster a sense of purpose and accomplishment.

7. Accept Imperfection:
    a. Recognize that nobody is perfect, and it's okay to make mistakes.
    b. Learn from your mistakes and view them as opportunities for growth.

8. Seek Professional Support:
    a. If self-esteem issues are deeply rooted or challenging, consider seeking guidance from a therapist or counselor.

9. Spiritual Practices and Prayer:
    a. Incorporate spiritual practices, such as prayer or meditation, to connect with a higher purpose.
    b. Reflect on your values and beliefs to find meaning and direction in your life.

Acknowledgement

The amount of support I've had along my journey in life, is a mirror reflection of how kind the world is. This book serves as a reflection of the self-worth I had to discover in a period over three years. My journey began in 2020 and self-worth at a root level was discovered in 2023. The women, men, communities and books that shaped me during this time still leave me in awe. I have so many gifted mentors who played an instrumental role in speaking, pouring, and shaping me in areas I never realized needed molding. I'd like to thank the following mentors, for sparking my inner flame. To Melanie Vogel, your willingness to be vulnerable forever changed me. David Bell, you saw something in me that I'm finally seeing. Dr. Stephanie Shipp, our bold conversations helped me identify clear actions towards my purpose. Reshenda Daniels, for showing me black excellence and introducing me to so many people who have positively impacted my life. To Olanda Sharp-Buckley, your sisterhood and mentorship means everything. I am grateful for how you show up for me, and how you remind me that God is always in control.

Many thanks to all of my mentors, I will never forget the time you spent sharing your stories that helped to shape mine. You have all been a Godsend.

Meet the Author

Consider this your first step towards your dream life. I will take you through my personal journey, one that took three years to get me to a place I call self-worth.

I wrote this book, so you too can have my personal formula for finding your self-worth. I am no stranger to helping. My core strengths are connecting and teaching. I earned my Bachelor of Science in Business Administration with a focus in Management. As I started my career, I realized how much I enjoyed talent and development, which inspired me to return to school for my Masters in Human Resources. I only worked in HR for two years—but that's a whole story for another book. I am an award-winning IT professional with over fifteen years of experience, specializing in global strategic initiatives and technical program management. Beyond my professional achievements, I've been awarded the opportunity to mentor junior and mid-career professionals, including friends and family. The strategies I've shared have resulted in promotions, new jobs and stronger leadership relationships.

I am passionate about partnering with others to achieve their success, while empowering them in their career journey.

My voice has been invited to moderate many industry-leading conferences, including: Tech in Motion and Business Leaders in Tech

(Diversity Conference). I've led an annual Executive Speed Coaching event for ten years, introducing employees to senior leadership for instant 1:1 coaching, impacting over six hundred people.

I hope this journal inspires you to live the life of your dreams, because you are worthy!

Final Thoughts of my Creative Process

As I turn to complete my last page, I'm greeted with an 11:11pm on the clock and on page 66 of 66. Cheers to the aligned moment of 11:11 that reminds us we are exactly where we're meant to be, and to the healing vibration of 66/66 that teaches us love, harmony and wholeness.

This book is dedicated to every soul who chooses to reclaim their voice, walk in their truth, and live unmuted. May these words guide you back to yourself and forward into your divine purpose.

For more details: Learn more by visting:www.thatunmutedlife.com or see QR code on the book back cover.

www.ingramcontent.com/pod-product-compliance
Lightning Source LLC
Chambersburg PA
CBHW031234120626
46545CB00003B/1118